STAGE
DIRECTION
Stories from a Passion Play

STAGE
DIRECTION
Stories from a Passion Play

RACHEL
KERR

Published by:
Quite Genuine Press
603 Pleasure Rd.
Lancaster, Pennsylvania 17601

Editing by Paul Schwartz
Cover design © 2016 by Think Cap Studios
Author photograph © 2016 by Laura Gandy Photography

Scripture quotations are from *The Holy Bible, English Standard Version*® (ESV ®), copyright © 2001 by Crossway, a publishing ministry of Good News Publishers. Used by permission. All rights reserved.

Published 2016
Printed in the United States of America

ISBN 978-0-692-73687-6
Library of Congress Control Number: 2016950966

TABLE of
C O N T E N T S

A Note from the Author

Acknowledgements

About the Author

A NOTE FROM THE AUTHOR

On May 19, 2013, one hundred thirty people, representing thirty-three different local churches, performed a passion play on the downtown streets of Elizabethtown, Pennsylvania.

Let's just marvel at that statement for a moment.

These were Christians from thirty-three different churches of all different denominations, working together in unity, without rivalry or petty debates. That kind of thing can only be credited to God's Holy Spirit helping Christians love each other in Jesus' name. There is no other explanation! Everyone agreed that Jesus' life and his gospel had to be shared with their city, so they devoted themselves to making this play happen.

They started from scratch, writing their own script, creating their own music, and tailoring their own costumes. It was a serious undertaking that all sprung from one man's vision—a vision that had been brewing for twelve years prior to the performance! A few professionals lent their skills to this project, but the people making it happen were generally amateur actors, and your average churchgoers. Still they took this creative work seriously and prepared each week for four months, sacrificing plenty of their nights and weekends to make this an excellent production. Their expression of their Savior was worth the time it took to do it well.

Their hard work wasn't wasted. Two thousand people stood in the audience on the day of the performance!

This day was the climax of all their efforts, and many of the stories you'll read here focus on that anticipated day. Yet even more of the stories took place in the months of preparation, while they were eating together, praying together, and wrestling with their roles. Some of the stories are more miraculous, and might have made me feel a bit skeptical—except they were told to me by honest people and confirmed by all. Other stories are more the everyday kind, but in a quieter way still show God to be real, personal, and influential in his followers' lives.

I didn't know this group of beautiful souls at the time of the Elizabethtown Passion Play. It took a lot of catching up in order to tell their stories.

I did dozens of interviews in order to learn their stories and tell them accurately. And I'll admit: the chance to be encouraged was why I agreed to compile their snippets of biography. I wanted a reason to sit down with each of these actors, musicians, and behind-the-scenes laborers, and hear real stories of how they experienced God in this event. Doing so changed me for the better, as I'd expected it would.

Here is just a sampling of the stories that most struck me. Each chapter is a different person's story, so you'll notice that instead of the stories being perfectly chronological, some of the events overlap. I could have written thirty more chapters on all the ways God showed himself in this passion play, but I opted to be brief and share what I felt were some of the highlights.

In listening to these stories and seeing the sincerity in each person's eyes, I saw my own faith growing. Their stories further convinced me that God is alive and active. I believe they'll do the same for you.

Chapter One
Phill
The Vision

Twenty years before the outdoor passion play in Elizabethtown, Pennsylvania, a similar play took place in downtown Lancaster, just a couple towns away.

"Alright, looks like it's showtime." Phill Stumpf looked up at his friend dressed in costume and mounted on one of the thieves' crosses. "You'll do great, Steve. But if you want to be convincing, stop grinning!"

It was a gray day during the Easter season in 1993, and Phill was only twenty-four years old. He'd gotten connected to the group performing the Lancaster Passion Play and attended a few of their prayer meetings in the last several weeks. In the meetings, Phill had prayed in faith that God would soften those in the audience who'd been hardened against Jesus and his gospel. He'd prayed for the crowd without thinking he'd be standing there with them, experiencing Jesus' story himself as if for the first time.

The other actors had just finished performing Jesus' trial scene in the center square, and the few thousand people who'd gathered to watch were now following as Jesus dragged his cross to the crucifixion site one block away. Phill found his perch on top of a brick wall and pushed his hands into his jacket pockets for warmth. Here he would have a nice view over the crowd.

At the crucifixion site, the audience watched in somber silence as soldiers mounted Jesus on the cross, mocking him the whole time. They abused and wounded him, and at the end of the heartbreaking scene, the narrator quoted, "Jesus cried out, 'It is finished!'"

It was then that heaven provided its own theatrical touch.

The sky was completely overcast, but in the moment that the Jesus character died, sunlight shone directly onto his face, and yet nowhere else. It was a heavenly spotlight. The moment felt supernatural, possibly meant to accentuate the drama. The play went on to show Jesus' burial and resurrection, all reenactments of miraculous events. There was so much awe in seeing the story. But what Phill couldn't stop thinking about was how heaven had just illuminated Jesus on the cross, and how the moment had further convinced him that the real Jesus was the Son of God, and very much alive. Jesus was not only alive, but involved in their telling of his story. The scene moved him so much that, decades later, Phill still sometimes replayed it in his mind.

——————

Nine years later, Phill sat in an Easter service at Elizabethtown Alliance Church. As Pastor Jim preached about Jesus' death and resurrection, Phill's memory flashed back to that overcast day on the square, and to how he suddenly better understood this Son of God in a human body. And there in his usual spot on his usual pew, Phill had an unusually unshakeable idea. God told him then that there would be a passion play on the main streets of E-town, with all the local churches involved. These thoughts kept coming to mind—"passion play," "main streets of E-town," and "all the churches involved"—in such a way that he suspected the idea was from God. Phill held on to what he believed God told him, and he prayed.

For ten years Phill waited, sharing his vision occasionally with pastors and friends, and praying about it. Understandably, he got discouraged from time to time, praying, "Is this of you, God? I don't want to confuse your will with my own feelings, or get in the way of what you want to do. Please, God... bring the people I need to accomplish this." But during these low points, God would always affirm Phill's vision, so he kept waiting and praying.

For those ten years, Phill assumed he would just serve as the visionary. He thought it was only a matter of finally meeting the right person, who would have the right skill set to put into motion such a big idea. It seemed like someone with plenty of theater experience, or resources, or excellent leadership skills would be right for heading up the Elizabethtown Passion Play. But God didn't want someone with five degrees in theatrical performance to initiate it. God wanted Phill Stumpf, a building material salesman, and the likeminded, mostly inexperienced actors who joined him. God picked Phill, of all people, to lead. He still chuckles at this now—at the irony of how God carries out his plans, and gives to his people whatever they lack.

Within two more years, they would block off the main streets of Elizabethtown, Pennsylvania, and draw the city into the drama of Jesus' life, death, and resurrection.

*For we are his workmanship, created in Christ
Jesus for good works, which God prepared
beforehand, that we should walk in them.*

EPHESIANS 2:10

Chapter Two
Ed
The Creative Touches

You should spend a little time with Ed Zeager. He's the kind of man who will fill your mind with questions and awe, and whatever he says will run through your mind for several days after. On the outside, he's a regular guy: a hardworking, teddy bear of a man who owns a landscaping company and resides in a wonderful old farmhouse. But getting to know him, you'll find he's a rare type. He'll tell you stories from his life that you wouldn't believe, except by the time you've heard a few of his stories, you've gotten to know him, and by then you know how sincere he is. He's lived what seems like too many miraculous stories for one man.

One of these miraculous events granted him the farmhouse he and his wife had been praying and aching to own for years. Once all the moving boxes were unpacked and they'd made the place their own, another miracle showed him exactly how to use the big stone barn on their new property. The building's layout was ideal for a live walk-through nativity! He and his family got to work staging the rooms in the barn, bought a donkey and some other animals to make the scenes feel real, and enlisted actors. That was twelve years ago now, and they've been putting on this live nativity every December. If you get to know Ed, you'll find out that this kind of thing, loads of work as it is, really feeds his soul.

Ed has always had an itch to show people who Christ is, and to do that outside of church walls. You could call it his passion, but that wouldn't be right. Really, it's his obsession. And he has new ideas brewing all the time. Over the years his live nativity has drawn thousands of people. Ed, being wired the way he is, is thrilled with the live nativity's success, but he's still aching to do more. It seems that God has put a holy restlessness inside him, one that for years and years no one seemed to quite understand, except his dear wife Vonnie. A calling that no one else seems to have can get a little lonely after a while, not to mention tiring.

But one January evening changed things for Ed. His friend Doug took him along to a meeting where a few people were going to talk about the dreams they had for ministry outside of church buildings.

There were others. Oh, after all this time, there were others!

By the time Doug dropped him off back at the farmhouse, Ed was so thrilled he could hardly stand it. Ed hustled out of the cold into the warmth of his home, and around the corner to the office, where his wife was typing. He burst out, "Vonnie!

You're not going to believe this. I've found people to join with." This might sound like a vague statement to anyone else, but Vonnie knew her husband, and she knew exactly what this meant.

They settled into the rocker and the recliner across from the wood burning stove, and turned off the television to give their full attention to the excitement at hand.

"The one fella's name is Phill, and he got to talking about how years ago God gave him a vision for a passion play on the streets of E-town. He said he knew it wouldn't be just one church putting it on. Can you imagine it, Vonnie?" Ed was smiling his biggest smile as he recapped the meeting for her.

Vonnie dreamed of the passion play along with Ed, and they chatted and imagined together until it was nearly midnight. Finally they climbed the creaky stairs to their bedroom.

Vonnie was ready to sleep, but Ed wasn't. How could he sleep? He was still wound up with excitement that he'd met other dreamers—and ones with dreams so similar to his own. What would happen next? What would God have them do as a team? It had been a profound night. God was planning big things, it seemed, and seeing this encouraged Ed tremendously.

Vonnie was sleeping, so as Ed lay beside her in the darkness, praying, he tried his best to be silent. He lifted his hands to heaven while he lay there in bed, praying and thanking God and shedding tears. In all that joy and gratitude he connected with God in such a way that he didn't think about time or bother to look at the clock. When he finally checked, it was 3 a.m. Ed finally dozed off.

At 6:45 a.m., Ed's alarm went off, and while he woke up with the memory of the ecstatic evening he'd had, he also remembered having a vivid dream. You could call it a vision.

In the vision, a dense crowd had gathered to watch the passion play on Main Street in Elizabethtown. The actors were showing what Jesus' trial might have been like, when another actor dressed as Satan slinked onto the street from between two buildings Ed recognized as being located on Main Street. And here's when the vision became confusing: Satan had brought a bubble wand with him and was blowing bubbles out into the crowd. Soon he was passing out bubble wands to anyone in the crowd who'd join him, trying to create a big, childish diversion while the Lord was being sentenced to death.

Ed needed help working through this one. He and Vonnie sat at the little table in the farmhouse kitchen and talked about the dream over their jelly toast and cup after cup of coffee. Ed means it when he says that Vonnie is his sounding board, and this was one of the most sobering things he'd needed her help with in quite a while.

Yes, it seemed like God had given him a scene for the passion play the same night that he'd learned about the idea. But Ed desperately wanted to be cautious. Was there any chance this was from Satan, meaning to weasel his way into the production and create a distraction in the script? He needed to be sure where the vision came from. All the excitement from the night before had given way to the seriousness of this new possibility.

For a week, the vision was all he could think

about, and Ed was constantly praying silent prayers, begging for God to make things clear. When there was a lull between his landscaping deliveries, Ed ducked into the big stone barn and stood all alone in the quiet. In the large, final room of the walk-through nativity, two massive wooden beams form a cross, and it stands in the barn year-round. Ed stood looking at it and asked again: "Lord, you know I don't mean no disrespect. I don't mean to question you. I think you understand... I just want to make sure this is right. Please if you could, make it clear to me. I need to know this was from you, and not from the enemy. Thank you, Lord."

When the week was over, another night's sleep brought another vision. Again a crowd was gathered on Main Street to watch the passion play being performed. Again it was a tragic point in the performance. The audience followed this time as the man portraying Jesus struggled to carry his own cross down the street toward the area where they would depict the crucifixion. He had been struggling for quite some time. When the cross once again slipped from his hands and his body collapsed onto the road, the mother of Jesus couldn't stand it, and ran out of the crowd to him, crying. Just then Satan crept out from the crowd and into everyone's view. This time he'd brought dead roses, and as he circled Jesus, he dropped them all around him. When he was finished, he flung the rest of his dead flowers into the crowd for dramatic effect. The look on his face was smug, like he knew Jesus' fate was bleak.

When Ed woke in the morning from this dream, he was confident that these two scenes—with their artistic interpretation of Jesus' story—

were not his, and not the enemy's. They were no one else's by God's. And God had given Ed the go-ahead by showing him a second scene meant for the passion play!

———

Ed, along with a few other guys who claimed they knew nothing whatsoever about writing—and especially nothing about script writing!—started meeting to work on the play's script. After all, they couldn't make much headway with casting for the play if they didn't have a script to start with! By May they had met three times and put a few scenes onto paper.

Then one morning that same May at 4:00 a.m., Ed woke up with lines running through his mind. The lines rhymed like a poem, and seemed to be something that belonged to the passion play. In fact, they seemed to be lines for the centurion to recite as he led the way to the crucifixion site. *I better jot this down after the alarm goes off*, Ed thought, and pulled his covers tight around him. But when the lines kept coming in a steady stream for another ten minutes, he knew he couldn't wait until it was time to get up. If he waited, he'd risk forgetting them altogether.

Ed pulled himself out of bed and made his way downstairs to the dining room. He clicked on the radio and let it play praise songs quietly in the background. The sky was dark outside, and everything was still, silent and reverent. Ed sat down at the simple wooden table, said a prayer that connected him to God, and started to write.

Yes, these lines would be perfect for the

centurion to speak as he ushered Jesus down the road with his cross. The centurion's character was calloused on the outside, barking at Jesus to get up every time he stumbled with the cross. But underneath that cruelty, were there questions? Did he wonder what kind of terrible mistake he would be making if this man was actually the Son of God? The poem gave a voice to that uncertainty.

Ed didn't think through what he was writing, and only paused a couple times to check whether or not the lines rhymed. The closer and closer he got to the end of the poem, the more obvious it became that it wasn't something he'd created. The last two paragraphs flew onto the paper.

He dropped his pen. "Where in the world did that come from?" he asked out loud. He was understandably stunned at what had just happened. He knew the answer to his question, of course. He took this miracle as another bit of reassurance that God wanted to see this play come together. They weren't doing this all alone, a team of humans with their human abilities only. God would help them the whole way through this giant task of creating an outdoor passion play from scratch. Anyway, it was God's adventure.

When Ed took the poem to the rest of the script-writing team, they couldn't wait to work it into the play. The only trouble with the poem was that it needed to be changed to a different verb tense, but Ed was glad that by editing, the other guys were able to take part in it.

The centurion's poem, along with the two scenes that Ed dreamed, appeared in the final performance of the Elizabethtown Passion Play.

ACT II

Scene 1: Carrying the Cross

SETTING: Several towers line the street with banners along them declaring sins in red. SOLDIERS put the cross on Jesus' back and shove him along his way. JESUS collapses along the way, and the SOLDIERS roughly prod him on. Here is where he looks up and changes the first of the towers from sin to white. During the following poem, the soldiers' actions will follow the words.

CENTURION 2

(watching Jesus, who is looking up)
It seemed like a fairly normal day,
Early one afternoon, you see,
Staring down a country lane,
Far South of Galilee.
The sun faded, behind the clouds to stay,
In the shadow of the city, it became clear to me. These people were angry, some seemed insane, Others celebrated with joy, but who is he? His clothes were in strips, with some torn away, A soldier's spear pierced his body. He looked over at me. My heart of stone could sense his pain.
The soldiers were whipping.
Would I set him free?
They'd placed a huge timber on his back to stay.
I thought, "How much weight must that be?"
His legs bent downward, his face showed pain.
One of my men spat on him, then there were three.

24

The torture seemed so relentless.

Why was it different today?

It now seems so senseless to me.

The question that lingers is still the same.

Could this man be the Christ? Could it be he?

Chapter Three
Matt
The Music

It hit hard when Earl told them. The play's director and script-writing team had gathered around the table at Ed's farmhouse to glean from the experience Earl Grove had working with Sight and Sound, a large local theater that performs biblically based productions. So when Earl told them they'd have to forget about using all the contemporary Christian songs they'd already written into the script, everyone was stunned.

But Earl was right. To go the route of using popular music in an open-air setting would require too much money for royalties and too much time to get approval. The resources just weren't there, and they didn't want to push back the performance date. The only practical thing to do was to, well, change everything.

Cutting out these songs would mean altering the entire script—and they were so close to being finished with the writing!

The group faced shock and discouragement as they brainstormed what to do next. Of course there would have to be music. A drama without music feels flat—it wouldn't be much of a play without it. Even for the viewer who pays no real attention to music, it undoubtedly sets the play's mood and carries the plot along. Where would they find music, then? They knew it would have to be completely original. They would need a composer.

Two musicians, Megan Straight and Pastor Jim Moynihan, were sympathetic to the situation and wrote a couple of songs each for the play's soloists. This was a great start, but the play was still left with no background melodies. Could a talented musician take on the rest of this project?

A worship leader who wasn't able to commit to the project himself recommended Matt Cassidy, a highly skilled musician with a degree in music education. At first glance, his taking on this project may have looked insane: now there were only four months left until the big performance, and Matt's life was already a balancing act of the Army National Guard, pilot obligations, full-time evening shifts, caring for his one-year-old son during the daytime, and finishing up graduate school. He would never have time to create the volume of music they needed!

Except that the very next month, Matt would have the perfect opportunity to devote himself to crafting the music. Matt was to travel to Fort Rucker, Alabama for an Aviation Maintenance Officers course during all of February and March. He would be free from his usual obligations, and from what he'd heard, he could expect to have plenty of downtime there to create music. The timing of this course was ideal, and nothing short of God-ordained!

Matt had actually done his helicopter training there at Fort Rucker, so the base was familiar to him. There he had musical friends he knew would be willing to loan the equipment and instruments he needed to record. Matt knew he could record with software instruments as needed, but recording live instruments was his preference. While at Fort Rucker, Matt was able to borrow drums, congas, a mandolin, a bass guitar, an acoustic guitar, and an electric guitar with an effects pedal. Conveniently, Matt's friend Jorge was the resident worship leader and had a key to the chapel on base. He gave Matt full access to the building for playing and recording. It was alone on the stage in that empty chapel that Matt did most of his work for the play.

Matt knew he had two months, and only two months. If he didn't finish the music for the play before he returned home, his other responsibilities would crowd out the work, and what was left simply wouldn't be done on time. So with this deadline in mind, he pushed himself hard. All his free time at Fort Rucker (thankfully, the rumors were true—there was plenty of free time!) was devoted to creating music for the passion play.

He created all original compositions that sound like a modern film score. What he wrote could be classified as new concert music, quite different from the contemporary Christian songs originally written into the play, and in the end, far better than what they'd originally planned!

For instance, the song composed for the trial

scene used eerie, dissonant strings to communicate tension, and it borrowed techniques from the early twentieth-century Twelve Tone composers. For the scene in which Jesus would carry his cross down High Street, Matt composed a song purposely reminiscent of the music he'd heard in *The Passion of the Christ.* The song's dramatic percussion (some of it actually the sounds of Matt playing the inside of a desk drawer) told the audience that the action was moving toward a climax. The epic quality of this song may have reminded listeners of the background music playing throughout many modern video games. And for the scene where Jesus would be taken off the cross, Matt composed a Baroque-inspired string melody that, in his words, was "solemn but gorgeous." The passion play's leadership team was getting far more than they'd even asked for! God had given them someone who took the job very seriously and refused to send them any half-hearted work.

So there would be no waiting, Matt shared the song files with the others back in Elizabethtown as soon as he completed each one. He wanted them to have all the time they could to practice and memorize. Meanwhile in Elizabethtown, Matt's talented friend Audrey Bloemendaal became the play's choir director, led the soloists' auditions, and continued to lead practices with the new music as they received it. Matt was grateful for her presence in Elizabethtown; their partnership in this project made everything fall into place.

Matt was working at an unusually quick pace, and yet turning out beautiful completed compositions. Typically, creating, recording, and polishing a song could take him anywhere between four and forty hours of hard work. But during those two months at Fort Rucker, he worked much faster and was able to create a volume of music he knew really should have taken him a year or more to complete. He completed fourteen different songs for the play in his two months there. It was a miraculous output of music! As Matt completed the last songs and shared them with the group, he and everyone back in Elizabethtown breathed a heavy sigh of relief.

Matt already had written more than four albums of music on his own, and two were for sale online, but often he had no contact with those who bought his music. He hadn't had the chance to see firsthand the impact of his creativity on the listener, and to know that God had blessed someone through his work. It was a precious opportunity then, when, after experiencing the passion play's performance from his spot in the sound booth, Matt was able to lead the worship service following the play. Among the songs he sang were a few he'd written himself. It was an incredible honor to see the audience following the drama and then worshiping Christ, both aided by his music. Finally Matt saw it: the work of God was being worked out through him.

Chapter Four
Brian
The Discomfort Zone

Brian Harper wasn't the sort of man you'd expect to see pulling into the parking lot that day to audition. His wife describes him as the kind of man you'd find in a corner at a party, keeping to himself. He's naturally introverted, extremely quiet, and needs someone to draw him out of himself. He was *not* by any means a performer!

So when he decided to drive straight past the bridge instead of taking his normal route, it was only because a spiritual dynamic was at work. In fact, he was so out of his comfort zone that he sat in his car for a while, telling God how stupid it was that he was there, about to audition. God didn't let up, though, and Brian lost the argument pretty quickly. He knew God was telling him to do an uncomfortable thing. He knew he had to go inside.

Brian was forty-nine years old and hadn't acted since first grade. He took a pen and filled out the form they handed him, which included a blank for his requested role. He wrote, "Whatever. Jesus," not expecting to win any part at all, but trying to be obedient to the Lord. For the audition, he read lines as Caiaphas the high priest, and also some lines as Jesus. Donna, the director, prompted him, "Could you try to be a little louder? And let's hear some emphasis!" Brian did the best he could, but he wasn't enjoying this. He hated having to stand up and perform in front of a crowd. When he left that day, he knew nothing would come of it.

When both sessions of auditions were through and Brian read the email from the director, he was shaking all over. It said that he was cast as Jesus. He'd landed a role? And it would be...Jesus? Brian's wife, Lisa, took a look and said, "Wow. Really?" Jesus. The role with the most lines, to be performed in front of thousands of people. Was there any other situation in which Brian could be more the center of attention? He was already fidgety and pacing around the room from the overwhelming nerves. They chose *him* to portray Christ? It was daunting. It was humbling. It was shocking. Most of all, it was scary.

Brian sensed that God meant for him to have this role, and as much as he wanted to, Brian couldn't argue this time. Deep down he knew God had been preparing him for this. For the past several years Brian had been traveling regularly to Nicaragua, to a mountain town on the jungle's edge. There he'd worked on water filtration projects and had gotten to know many of the people, and many pastors. God had shoved Brian out of his comfort zone through his friendship with one particular pastor, who one time had given Brian five minutes' notice that he was about to be interviewed on the radio. Another time that same pastor had given Brian five minutes' notice that he was about to bring a message at a house church. Moments like this were quite a feat for Brian, and had him fidgety and pacing, nervously touching his face just like he was now. But God had brought him through those moments, and he'd preached in Nicaragua at least twenty times over the years! God would help him with the passion play, too, wouldn't he?

———

He set to work learning his host of lines. Brian would pace the floor in his warehouse apartment and stare out the huge windows as he recited them. In the shower every morning, too, he was focused, working on his lines. The memorization itself was such a big job that he couldn't internalize the lines for a while; they were just recited words. But as the words began to flow out automatically, he felt the emotions to match, and began to understand more of the abandonment Christ experienced.

Even in the practices, Brian began to feel some of the abuse Jesus felt. Brian had to endure beatings and rough treatment throughout every run of the script. It was physically hard for him to get through the rehearsals. The strikes were fake, of course, but when the guards did their best to make the beatings appear real, Brian inevitably suffered some scrapes and bruises. The guard's whip left marks and even broke skin during one lashing. It was a small but sobering taste of Jesus' punishment.

The day of the play, Brian was pacing and fidgeting more than ever. He prayed as he paced: *Lord, I'm terrified. You have to help me to do this. Please, God, help me! You know I can't do it myself.* The cast circled up backstage and prayed together just before the performance was to start. Praying with the other actors reassured Brian, but he didn't stop shaking. He was still shaking violently when he stepped onto the stage. But in the performance they'd been anticipating all along, Brian recited every line perfectly without missing a single word— the only time he'd done it perfectly beginning to end!

That day he felt Christ's rejection much more strongly than he had even in the practices. He felt it the most while he was struggling to carry the heavy cross down High Street, stumbling and only being shouted at, but never being helped, despite the thousands watching. The moment felt real for him. He couldn't understand perfectly what Christ endured, of course, but it was a powerful, painful experience for Brian. From then on, he had a much richer sense of Christ's passion.

Redemption came after the resurrection scene, when Brian trudged toward the dressing rooms and a crowd of about fifteen kids swarmed around him. A seven-year-old girl asked Brian if he would pray for her friend's broken arm, and another girl about the same age asked if he would pray for her friend whose parents were planning a divorce. A young woman with special needs joined the crowd with her mother by her side. The young woman was smiling a giddy smile, and hugged Brian. Brian bent down to chat with a four year old little boy, asking, "Do you know who Jesus is?" "Do you love him?" "Do you know that Jesus loves you?" He communicated Jesus' love to everyone in the group the best he could. To have their vulnerable attention was such a privilege. It was beautiful, and Brian's favorite memory of the play.

———

Weeks after performing the play, Brian was taking a shower and was several scenes into quoting his lines before he caught himself. He grinned. It had been such a habit to practice his lines there, and anywhere, in any free moment he had! He grinned, too, at the way God had taken his insecurity, and quietness, and even his imperfection, and used him anyway to communicate who his Son was in front of thousands right there in Elizabethtown. It was a crazy feat! But it wasn't such a feat for the Almighty.

———

Christ redeemed us from the curse of the law by becoming a curse for us—for it is written, "Cursed is everyone who is hanged on a tree"—so that in Christ Jesus the blessing of Abraham might come to the Gentiles, so that we might receive the promised Spirit through faith.

GALATIANS 3:13-14

He was despised and rejected by men; a man of sorrows, and acquainted with grief; as one from whom men hide their faces he was despised, and we esteemed him not. Surely he has borne our griefs and carried our sorrows; yet we esteemed him stricken, smitten by God, and afflicted. But he was pierced for our transgressions; he was crushed for our iniquities; upon him was the chastisement that brought us peace, and with his wounds we are healed. All we like sheep have gone astray; we have turned—every one—to his own way; and the Lord has laid on him the iniquity of us all. He was oppressed, and he was afflicted, yet he opened not his mouth; like a lamb that is led to the slaughter, and like a sheep that before its shearers is silent, so he opened not his mouth.

ISAIAH 53:3-7

Chapter Five
Deb
The Mother's Heart

Several Costa Rican women huddled around Deb Garber, lifting prayers in their best broken English. Over and over, they asked that she would have peace as she left her son Matt there in Costa Rica and returned home. All the while Deb was thinking to herself what sweet prayers they prayed—but they must not have known how much her son had traveled in the past. She and Matt had said many temporary goodbyes. This was just another on the list. Deb did have peace, but she was thankful for their kindness.

Matt and a Costa Rican friend insisted on going with Deb to the airport. The long drive there showcased the tropical landscape with all its mountains and farmland. Much of it looked like the farm on top of the high mountain where Matt would work the land during the day and retire to his humble living quarters at night. Matt was freshly graduated from Eastern Mennonite University and was planning to work in Lancaster General Hospital's emergency room at the end of the summer, but first he wanted to spend these few months serving the families he knew from a previous trip to Costa Rica. Deb was glad for him, that he would be spending the next three months living this simple life, plowing with oxen, tending to the goats, selling milk at the closest market, and loving the people there. Deb felt happy and peaceful.

She felt peaceful—and then the car turned into the lane next to the airport entrance, where she would be dropped off. Suddenly she found herself clutching her knees and fighting to hold in tears. *Am I going to cry?* she thought. Feelings of terror had come from nowhere, for no apparent reason.

Matt walked around the car to give her a big hug goodbye, and right away Deb was sobbing in his arms. She'd never cried this way before in her life! It was completely without restraint, without composure, and from a deep place inside her that she couldn't understand.

"Mom, what's wrong? Are you afraid to fly?" She wasn't sure what was wrong, and felt sorry for her son that she was making such a scene.

"No, Matt, I'm not afraid to fly. It's just going to be so long before I see you again," was her attempt at an explanation.

"It won't be long—only three months." Matt smiled and did his best to comfort her.

That's right, it's only three months! I don't know why on earth I'm so upset...

Deb took her suitcase, checked in, and found the waiting area, where she listened to a violinist playing and made small talk with a Spanish woman beside her. By the time she boarded her plane, she was calm again, but exhausted from all the emotion.

Two months passed. Matt happily integrated into the Costa Rican culture and called home regularly. Meanwhile, Deb was at peace. Her tearful incident at the airport had been a fluke. Then on July 1, 2008, as she drove home from work, that same mysterious sobbing came over her again, just as it had when she told Matt goodbye. Again the cries came from her deepest recesses—and yet she was unsure why she was crying. But when the phone call came that evening five hours later, she understood, and her entire family wept the same helpless way in their grief.

They had lost Matt to the Pacific Ocean.

——————

Losing a twenty-two-year-old son brings an unimaginable amount of pain. Deb can only try to describe the experience to someone who hasn't lived it. But she will assure you that God took care of her in it. For the amount of heartache she felt, God faithfully matched it with support, comfort, and even joy. Deb says that now she really knows what it means for the Holy Spirit to act as her Comforter, and is generally more aware of his invisible work.

During those first months of grief, friends and believers came out of the woodwork to support Deb and her family in visible ways, too. And even when she and her husband, Todd, traveled to Costa Rica one year later, she felt reassured of God's love. Being there could have felt like a punch in the stomach, but it wasn't at all—it was uplifting, actually. The residents who had known Matt had such beautiful things to say about him, telling stories that showed God had grown him in ways even his mother didn't know. Deb was grateful. The Lord was caring for her broken mother's heart.

It wasn't long before Deb was able to say with peaceful conviction that birth and death are both sacred and God-ordained.

———

Deb had done a lot of healing when, five years later, she heard about plans for the passion play in Elizabethtown. Even though common sense reminded her of her last experience with acting—when she had joined the community theater's cast of *The King and I* alongside Matt, but during the performance completely blanked on her one line!—still she felt drawn to the passion play. A part of her stalled and hesitated to audition, but an even bigger part couldn't ignore the opportunity. Matt had started piano lessons when he was just five years old, and as he grew older it became obvious how talented he was in music, and in drama as well. He starred in countless productions in his high school and college years. No doubt he would have jumped at the chance to be in this play. Since he couldn't audition, Deb would.

On her audition sheet Deb jotted down, "Mary, mother of Jesus" as her desired role. How could she not be drawn to the part of a mother losing her son?

The director liked the idea of Deb as the

mother of Jesus, too, so the role was hers. This meant she would be singing a solo of "Mary's Lullaby" near the cross and reciting some speaking lines, but not too many. This felt manageable to her, and gradually she got over her stage fright.

Deb had long been familiar with the gospel story, but she'd never given much thought to who Jesus' mother was and what she might have experienced. But now that Deb knew the ache of losing a child, too, she felt like she understood Mary in ways she hadn't before. And as she stepped into Mary's character over and over again for months of play practices, she couldn't help but meditate on Mary.

She remembered the story of Jesus' first public miracle: turning water into wine for a wedding reception in Cana. Interestingly, this is always called Jesus' first public miracle. But how many private miracles might he have done, and how much of his supernatural power had his mother witnessed in their home? In the story at Cana, Mary was fully confident in Jesus' power to help when the wine supply ran out. How had Jesus miraculously cared for his mother during their years together? Deb could only imagine!

Deb noticed she was also thinking differently about Jesus' resurrected appearance to Mary Magdalene. Mary Magdalene was the fortunate first person to see Jesus alive after his death. Deb hadn't thought much of this before, but now she found herself reacting, *Hey—why not appear to your mother first? I'd have been jealous!* She smiled, too, at the part when Jesus warned Mary Magdalene not to touch him. *It must have been much harder to keep his mom from hugging him when she saw him alive!* she thought.

There was a part of Deb that even envied Mary, since Mary was able to walk alongside her son in his most tragic hours, and Deb grieved the distance that had been between her and the Costa Rican shore that day. It made her think, too, what faith Mary must have had to go along in support of Jesus, knowing this cruel fate was divinely ordained and necessary for the world's salvation. How hard that must have been, and how strong Mary was to be there and agree with her son that this difficult thing was ultimately good.

Even though Deb had been sure she'd grieve for her own son while playing Mary, she found that months of meditation on Jesus' life left her grieving the world's loss of Christ in the flesh instead.

Still her personal loss had taught her how people weep in a tragedy. Because of the way she cried when she was acting, other cast members kept commenting on how convincing she was! They didn't know. She hadn't told any of them what had brought her to the passion play. The cast and crew were made up of people from all over Elizabethtown who attended different churches and generally didn't know one another outside of the play. No one had a clue about Deb's loss five years before.

On the day of the big performance, the cast and crew took time out from their preparations to eat a meal together under the big meeting tent. They passed a microphone from person to person while gathered there, and like the family they had become, they shared honest testimony after testimony. *It's time to tell them,* Deb thought. By this point she was starting to feel like she was carrying a burden secretly, and for no reason. When the microphone was finally in her hands, she took a breath and confessed the ache that had led her to pursue the play and her specific role. Instantly she felt relief! When someone else told her later that a personal loss had brought them to the play, too, she knew her vulnerability had been a good thing.

When the performance began, it wasn't long before Deb was drawn into the drama, as if she really was Mary, and it really was crucifixion day. She even felt protective motherly instincts toward Jesus as the guards abused him and the crowd sneered. But when she set those feelings aside, she found herself praying for the crowd as they all headed toward the cross. She wondered if the real Mary had risen above her natural reactions, too, and prayed for the crowds around her. Even on the day of the play, Deb was receiving new insight into Jesus' story by walking through it as his mother.

Birth and death are both sacred and God-ordained. Deb knew this in a deeper way after moving from her own loss to the loss of Christ in the passion story. And with a Father God so loving and so sovereign, redemption can always grow out of tragedy.

SCRIBE
So, Satan made all this happen?

JOHN
No, Jesus knew this was God's plan all along. He's in control of everything, no matter how out of control things may appear.

(As JESUS nears the stage, a SOLDIER stops him. SIMON passes him and drops the cross near the stage. SIMON runs back to his children while soldiers lift the cross onto the stage. Once it's in place, JESUS walks away from the soldiers and to the stage. Collapsing up the stairs, he crawls across the stage and lays himself on the cross. The SOLDIERS stand in awe a moment before stepping forward. The CENTURION hands them the bag Jesus had carried earlier. They use his own hammer and nails. They nail the sign to the cross.
Music plays. As they raise the cross, MARY makes her way near the front of the crowd with JOHN a little ways off. JESUS catches YOUNG JOHN's eye, then looks to Mary.)

JESUS
(to Mary)
Woman, behold your son.
(to Young John)
Behold your mother.

(YOUNG JOHN moves over to Mary and stands by her protectively.)

Chapter Six
Jack
The Healing

Jack Bezares is quite a storyteller. He's such a storyteller, in fact, that there can be no better way for someone to hear his story than to hear it in Jack's own words. I'm so convinced of this that I haven't written his story in my voice but have given it to you straight as I heard from him in our interview:

JACK: So first, I got hoodwinked into doing this. I was the last person to sign up to be an actor. Brian Harper was living in the same complex with me and approached me one evening and said, "Hey, have you heard about the passion play?"

"Oh yeah, they're going to do it right here in town, in May or something?"

"Yeah, yeah, they were asking for men to come help and I was thinking about you."

"Doing what?"

"Well, they need you to play a part."

"Oh, really? Well I hope it's not Jesus."

"No, I'm playing Jesus."

"Oh, okay, cool! That's just way too many lines for me to remember. So what's the part?"

"Oh, well, you're going to play [mumbles]."

"I'm sorry?"

"The bad thief."

"Dude, seriously? Last year I played Ashbenez as the antagonist in the Daniel story for VBS, so I was the village idiot, I was the anti-everything, and then they asked me, 'Can you help with the Christmas play?' 'Yeah, sure, what do you need?' 'Well, we need you to play Herod.' And now I'm the bad thief! Why am I typecast?" Maybe it's my pronunciation, because I'm from the Bronx.

So I started going, doing the practices and stuff, the fittings and things, and it was going pretty well. We had a number of times when we just got together and prayed away illnesses for people, who were down with a cold or something. And during all of this, I started to have a problem.

I had been in for a physical just before my 60th birthday. So I went to the doctor here at Norlanco, and the whole test, everything was fine, all the bloodwork came back. They said 'You've got the organs of a twenty-five-year-old, this is perfect. Just take an EKG on the way out.' I took the EKG and by the time I got back to my house, which is five minutes away, my phone's ringing.

"This is Norlanco. Do you know you've had a heart attack?"

"Wait—what?"

"Do you know you've had a heart attack?"

"I don't think I've had a heart attack."

"No, no, you've had a heart attack. We need you to see a cardiologist."

"Listen, every time I go to a doctor for a physical, I end up with five to ten thousand dollars' worth of tests, and it all turns out to be nothing."

"No, no, this is different. You really need to see a cardiologist."

"Well, I'm going to heaven. I'm not worried about it." The woman was confounded.

So by Sunday morning, it's sinking in: *Wait a minute. So I'm eventually going to die from this. Maybe not today. This isn't fun anymore.* I was getting very tired, very worn out. So then I called back and made the appointment to see the cardiologist.

They set me down for an echocardiogram, a stress test, so they take the ultrasound of your heart first, then they put you through the torture test until you hit your point on the incline plane. I was a medic, so I know what eyes look like when they're communicating back and forth, and I kept looking at this guy and looking at this girl and looking at this guy...so I said, "What's going on?"

"Oh, nothing, nothing."

So at the end they lay you down and they do it quickly. And they thought that an eighth of my heart muscle was necrotic, had died. That's why they thought I had suffered a heart attack, because it was deprived of oxygen long enough to kill it.

JACK'S WIFE: And this was on his birthday, that's where we spent his sixtieth birthday, was in the hospital.

JACK: Oh yeah, it was a grand surprise.

So they get done with that and they're giving each other that look.

"Seriously, what's wrong?"

"You have to talk to your doctor."

I'm supposed to get the results in a week or something. They called me the next day.

"You've got to come see the cardiologist again, we've got to set you up for another test." So then I had to go in for an angiogram the day after the passion play.

So all through this people at my church had been praying and did the laying on of hands. My brother's in the ministry, my dad's been on and off in ministries, and they all said the same thing when they prayed with me: "May God protect you," and at the end they would say, "May the doctors and the medical staff be confounded by this healing." I'm still not worried, I know I'm going to heaven, so I'm okay, I'm at peace.

So the day of the passion play we got together early on and stopped to have a break, eat some food, and we're fellowshipping, and the director tells me, "Hey, Jack, come here, sit down." Just pulled a chair out and I'm like, "What are we doing—let's beat up Jack?" And they started praying. There were about a hundred people I guess, between the actors and everybody, and they just went on and on and on. It was like the waiting room for heaven as far as I'm concerned! And they all prayed the same thing: "May the doctors wonder what happened that everything turned out well."

And by that time, I couldn't even walk 150 feet without panting. I was exhausted. I was just exhausted. When everyone met up at the crucifixion and resurrection scene and everyone else went down to mingle in with the crowds in costumes, I had to hang out at the cross—and I fell asleep on the cross waiting for them to come up because I was shot, just worn out.

So the next day we went in for the angiogram and I'm still walking into the hospital like it's my last mile. So it was about 45 minutes and I was awake through the whole thing and they said, "Okay, we're almost done here."

So I said, "Did you put any stents in?"

They said, "No."

I said, "Wait a minute, nothing? Did you knock something loose?"

"No," they said. "We checked, we went into every one of your coronary arteries and you have the smallest amount of plaque in there that we've ever seen in someone your age."

"Okay, so what caused this anomaly to show up in these multiple tests?"

And they kind of gave each other that look like, *We're going to charge this guy five grand and tell him, There's nothing wrong with you!* And they said, "There's nothing wrong with you, nothing at all—you're fine."

And when I got up, it was like I was twenty. I felt like the weight of the world was off my shoulders. They had to wheel me back, and you had to keep pressure on it for an hour or something like that because they had gone into the femoral artery, and then the nurse said, "Okay, sit up and I'm going to walk you around the ward a little bit because we have to make sure it holds."

"Okay, fine." So I took about three steps and I did a soft-shoe *ta-da* like this.

She said, "Don't do that!"

And I said, "I feel great!" I could have run a quarter mile easily. And they were all confounded. I kept saying, "What do you think caused the anomaly?"

"Well, we used better equipment this last time."

"No, I used a better doctor this last time, the Great Physician, the One and All."

That's my testimony. And I tell people that we should walk around as a lighted billboard for God, that we should be so happy that others should approach us, "What's going on with you, what have you got that I don't have?" I feel that that's our mission, and it's just been great ever since. So there it is, and life is wonderful all the time. It's a thing of beauty.

———

Bless the Lord, O my soul,
and all that is within me, bless his holy name!
Bless the Lord, O my soul,
and forget not all his benefits,
who forgives all your iniquity,
who heals all your diseases,
who redeems your life from the pit,
who crowns you with steadfast love and mercy,
who satisfies you with good
so that your youth is renewed like the eagle's.

PSALM 103:1-5

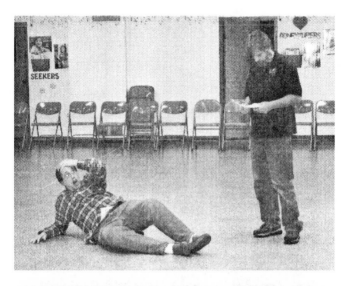

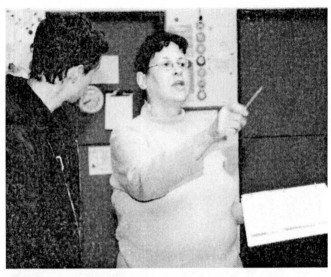

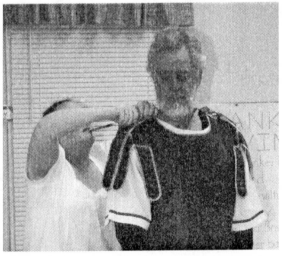

All photos used with permission.

Chapter Seven
Rob
The Date and Time

Rob Bustin stepped outside his apartment building onto the High Street sidewalk and followed it down toward Folklore, the trendy corner cafe. It was pretty convenient that he could easily stroll there anytime he started craving a mocha! His phone rang in his pocket, and he answered.

"Hi, Ed! How's it going?"

"Hey, Rob..." Rob slowed his pace. Two words in, and already Rob could tell something was wrong. Ed didn't sound like himself. "Rob, we have a bit of a problem."

"What's that?" Rob stood still in order to focus on what Ed was saying.

"Well, you know the borough council met today and talked about closing the street for the play...oh, I hate to say it, Rob, but they denied our permit."

"What?" Rob stared at the passing traffic in

a daze. It was this street, High Street, that they needed to be closed off for the passion play. "Ed, they denied it? You've got to be kidding! Why? What—what are we supposed to do?"

It was March, already *March*—and the play was in May! Both Rob and Ed were too upset to rally much hope over the phone. Rob stuffed his phone back into his pocket and kept moving.

This is a disaster! Two months before the play, and the borough isn't going to let us do it! What now, God? I mean, really, what now? He trudged the rest of the way to the cafe, pushed open the glass door, and fell into the first open seat. Rob just stared into the coffee rings on the table and thought spiraling, hopeless thoughts.

But, of course, the Holy Spirit didn't let him sulk for long. With just a couple of reminders of what he knew to be true about God, his reeling thoughts formed into a prayer: "God, I know you know what's going on, and you can move this mountain. Please, Lord, move it. We're really worried, but the truth is, this isn't too big a problem for you to handle. Please just...help."

Rob straightened and walked to the end of the line to order his mocha. Even though his spirit was encouraged and he was choosing to have faith in a big God, his frail humanity was still shocked and shaken. He jumped when his phone rang again. Again it was Ed.

"Hey, Rob. We got a meeting with Jack, the chief of police, tomorrow at one o'clock, in his office. I'd love for you to be there."

"Definitely, Ed! I'll make sure I'm there!"

Rob had started out as a member of the

script-writing team for the play, which had then morphed into the leadership team for the play. He hadn't expected this level of responsibility, and he didn't have much practice in leadership, but he considered it quite an honor. He'd arrange to work from home the next day so he could attend the meeting with Jack Mentzer, the chief of police. He wouldn't miss it for anything.

Promptly at 1 p.m. the next day, Rob, Ed, Phill Stumpf, Pastor Al Frank, and Pastor Doug Lamb filed down the hallway, following Jack to his office. Jack closed the door, and took his seat and a deep breath. When everyone had crowded in, he began to explain to the group that their biggest problem was Elizabethtown College's commencement ceremony, which would be May 18, the same Saturday they'd planned to perform downtown. Blocking a main street for eight hours that day simply was not going to work. How would graduation traffic move in and out of Elizabethtown? Besides, the college was so close to the heart of downtown, the band playing at the end of the ceremony would interrupt the play.

The chief of police was sincerely grieved to give them bad news again—he'd already had to break it to them that Market Street, their first choice, was off-limits, and they'd had to move the play's location to High Street, the second-busiest street downtown. Difficult as it was to have such a conversation again, they needed to know the play wasn't going to happen, unless they made a new plan for when and where.

It was time to brainstorm.

"We could do the play on that same day and just perform in a different place, maybe outside of town," someone suggested. Sure, the borough wouldn't have any problem with that, but all along God had been leading them to perform *downtown*. They shook their heads as they mulled it over. No, moving the play outside of town wasn't the answer.

"We could use a little side street that doesn't get much traffic," someone else offered. But that didn't quite feel right, either. They all agreed that they felt as if God wanted them to be smack dab in the middle of town—perfectly visible, impossible to miss, on a main street. Pastor Doug's arms were folded tight, and you could see his righteous anger stewing below the surface. Pastor Al's gestures were becoming more and more dramatic as he chimed in.

"Okay. What if we kept the same location but just changed the date? How about the weekend before?" But that was Mother's Day weekend. That was no good.

"Well, then the weekend after." Except that the weekend after was nearly June, and people would be leaving town for their first vacations of the summer. None of these suggestions felt like the solution. Ed sat in his chair with shoulders slumped, looking absolutely defeated.

On the outside they were scrounging for solutions, but inside everyone was having the same fearful thoughts. They were wondering if the entire play, and all the work they'd done up to this point, was going to fall through. The suggestions stopped. It was an impasse. The room was quiet.

"You'd be welcome to do the play on Sunday. You wouldn't have any traffic issues then...but that would probably conflict with your Sunday services," the chief of police said.

Sunday. *Sunday.* Why not Sunday?

There was a pause. Suddenly every man in the room felt hope again, just as if the Holy Spirit had dropped it into them at once.

"Yeah, why not Sunday?" Phill blurted out, and the discussion resumed with a brand-new energy. The chief of police wiped away a tear from his eye. He felt such relief that his bad news hadn't been the play's ruin!

Phill and Rob immediately stepped into the hallway to make phone calls. They couldn't be sure that they'd found the solution until they knew that the director, the cast, and everyone else was available to perform on Sunday instead. Rob phoned Donna, the director, first, and was thrilled to hear that she could be there to direct on Sunday. The others sat inside Jack's office, jittery with anticipation, while Phill and Rob called everyone they could think of.

When they finally stepped back inside, they announced it: "Sunday's going to work!"

What an emotional swing they'd all felt—from despair to euphoria! Praise God! He still intended for the play to happen.

———

On May 18th, the Saturday that was the original date for the play, the cast gathered in costumes for their dress rehearsal outside at the industrial park, which was the best outdoor space they could find resembling High Street. The weather forecast was stormy, but they had prayed that God would hold off the rain until their practice was over. They got through the script once, but before they could run through a second time, rain started to pour, despite their prayers.

The group moved to the Elizabethtown Alliance Church basement to finish their practice, where they quickly discovered that an upstairs toilet was overflowing, causing water to pour down through the ceiling below.

Rob knew it was too coincidental. The rain had started exactly when the play would have begun if they'd kept the play's original date. Weather would have ruined the play if they hadn't changed the date to Sunday. And if the rain hadn't moved their rehearsal to the church, the water damage inside would have been far worse by the time someone found it.

Rob noticed a stage hand wearing one of the passion play's promotional shirts that had been printed before the date was changed. "May 18" was crossed out in permanent marker and re-written "May 19." Rob shook his head and smiled, amazed. God has the best plans.

The heart of man plans his way, but the Lord establishes his steps.

Proverbs 16:9

Chapter Eight
Sonya
The Performance

High Street was bustling and packed tight with onlookers. Today was the day. Yes, *the* day. May 19 had finally come!

The cast had practiced outdoors a handful of times, but they had never practiced on the street where the play would actually take place. Actually, most of their practices had been in a church basement, where they'd used a lot of imagination to climb invisible steps onto an invisible stage. They'd walked laps around the big room as if walking one long, straight stretch down High Street toward the crucifixion site. This kind of situation left a lot of uncertainty. They'd had hopes of practicing on High Street early in the day, but time was running out, and they were already drawing an audience. They made a quick decision to save it for the actual performance and to just pray, pray, pray for grace to perform well.

Every actor, choir member, sound tech, and stage hand could feel the anticipation. Pastor Al was speaking his introductory lines as Sonya Pena picked up the hem of her angel's robe and ascended the steps to the stage. Hers were the first true lines of the play, and she had plenty of lines. She had paragraphs to remember.

The last handful of practices leading up to the play had had Sonya's stomach in knots. When the other actors were struggling with their lines in the very last practices, Sonya was worried for them, but she was worried for herself too. *What if I forget my lines? What if I mess up right at the beginning, and that spoils everyone else's confidence? And then the rest of the play is ruined! Oh, I can't mess up! Lord, please help us.*

Once the emcee focused the crowd's attention, Sonya took the stage. And in the pit of her stomach she felt it.

Sonya felt that the thousands of people she saw packed into the street before her, representing Elizabethtown, needed to know her Savior, Jesus. There were more of them than she'd expected, and they were a striking image. She felt the history she had with the town and with this particular street, the one she drove to school for years. She felt that many of the faces in that sea of people must have been in her high school yearbook, or clerks she'd bought from, or parents she'd worked with. She felt that any of these familiar faces who didn't know she was identified with Jesus, well, they would soon know.

She felt the weight of that many souls

standing in High Street, about to give attention to Jesus' story.

Here goes.

Sonya stood in her white robe and her enormous feathery wings and spoke her lines as an angel as best she could. And to her relief, the lines delivered themselves in the way that lines usually do when they've been practiced so many times. *Thank you, Father! Oh, thank you, Lord!*

She hurried off toward the dressing room when she was finished. As she listened to the scenes following hers, she was thrilled to hear everyone delivering their lines better than they'd ever done in the practices! Sonya ducked into the basement of the Lutheran church and as fast as she could, changed from an angel into a mourner. She swapped her angelic robe for a commoner's clothing, rubbed on some makeup to appear a little more Jewish, and rushed to catch up to the other mourners.

Sonya was quickly back on the street and blending in with the crowd. As she walked, she noticed the somber gray sky they had as their backdrop, and even more people watching the performance from so many of the windows lining the street.

It wasn't long before Sonya's two-year-old son Ian, who was there in the crowd watching the performance, was asking for her. Sonya picked him up, he in his cowboy T-shirt and sneakers, she in her period costume, and they followed Jesus and his cross together. Still she was deep in character, and feeling the weight of the events they were acting out.

Sonya was drawn into the moment, shouting, "No! Don't do this! He doesn't deserve it!" as others shouted, "Crucify him!" and as the Roman guards roughly pushed back the crowd pressing in toward Jesus. It wasn't forced acting anymore, not for Sonya and not for anyone else. Everyone there was swept away in the scene. Sonya was genuinely mourning, shedding real tears. So were many in the audience.

In practices, all she'd felt was a concern that everyone would forget their lines when the day of the play finally came. And how stressful it was to know they couldn't run through the performance on that particular street until showtime! But on this day that they'd anticipated for a full year, that anxiety fell away, and the drama had a power it hadn't had in the practices. To Sonya, it truly felt as though she was there on the day Jesus was being crucified.

Sonya wasn't the only one sensing this. Amid the crowd of actors and spectators that were mixing in, there were countless sober expressions. More and more people leaned out of second-story windows to watch. Two middle-aged women kept close to the action the whole time, raising their hands in worship, crying, and even kneeling from time to time. It was difficult to not be moved.

There were a couple of sound glitches during the play, which could only be expected when this was the first ever run-through with the microphones (which at some points had to pick up a signal from 800 feet away!), but Sonya describes these moments as listening to a sermon preached in a foreign language. Even if the listeners missed some words here and there, the overall message and its tone still seemed to come across loud and clear.

Throughout the play Sonya's husband, Horeb, stayed closer than anyone to the action in order to capture video of the performance. Even though Horeb wasn't familiar with the script at all, the Lord allowed him to be positioned in just the right spots at just the right moments. He filmed several shots that captured the rich, rich emotion of the scene. One was when Simon of Cyrene was finished carrying Jesus' cross for him, and he and his son were separated, searching for each other in the crowd. In Horeb's shot, their troubled expressions and the actors swarming around them showed perfectly the sense of confusion, making the event feel very real.

When the crucifixion scene came, Sonya was still holding Ian, and she quickly covered his innocent eyes. She wasn't sure how much of the play he understood, but she wanted to shield him from some of the brutality. Later Ian would announce his plans to use his toy sword to "beat up the guys that were hurting Jesus." He was only two, but he was certainly absorbing Jesus's story that day.

It was ironic—all along, Sonya and the whole cast and crew had hoped for a bright, sunny day for their performance, but God knew better. He allowed a somber gray sky that would reinforce the gravity of Jesus' mistreatment and death. That gray sky also served as the perfect backdrop for another of Horeb's shots. When Jesus' dead body was being carried from the crucifixion site to the tomb, Horeb captured it perfectly from a low angle so that it was all despair and gray sky.

When the burial and resurrection scenes

were finished and the play was done, the two middle-aged women who had responded so emotionally all throughout the play approached Sonya.

"You have such a powerful church!" they told her.

"You know this isn't just my church..." Sonya explained. "This is about thirty different churches working together." She realized how surprising it sounded when she said it.

"Wow. Oh! Oh, wow!" The women were dumbfounded by what they'd seen and heard. Sonya never forgot them or how strongly they responded to the performance. God was at work.

Sonya's concern for months had been that the people of the town would be irritated by the passion play. They were, after all, creating a pretty big inconvenience by blocking off a main downtown street for several hours. Traffic nuisances like this *always* make people angry, don't they? All Sonya and the others could do was pray for a good response to the play.

The next day everyone reading the morning paper in Elizabethtown and in nearby Lancaster saw this prayer answered. There were spectacular photos of the crowded street and even a portrait shot of Sonya as the angel. And every bit of the press coverage was positive. Even more amazing than this was that the city later reported that there wasn't a single complaint—not a single one!—about the street being blocked during the play.

God's grace generously covered the details of that day for Sonya and the others, and certainly that same grace was felt by everyone watching with an open heart.

Today: Thunderstorm, 79.
Tonight: Thunderstorm, 62.
Tuesday: Thunderstorm, 87.
Details: The Back Page.

LANCASTERONLINE.COM

LAN

Local

Par

Big par
school:

BY

gsn

When
out her da
lunchtime
she was f

Not ne
who has
is a spe
Manhei
Rather,
school,
the de
ered a
princi

**E-town Passion Play
draws 2,000 people**

About 2,000 people packed
East High Street in
Elizabethtown Sunday as the
borough hosted a huge
production of the Passion Play.
Page B1

For I am not ashamed of the gospel, for it is the power of God for salvation to everyone who believes, to the Jew first and also to the Greek.

ROMANS 1:16

Chapter Nine
Pastor Jim
Prodding and Obedience

"Hi, welcome! It's good to have you. Will you be auditioning for acting or singing, or both?"

Jim Moynihan found himself there on the piano bench leading auditions for the upcoming passion play, the very same auditions he'd been sure he wasn't going to attend.

He stacked a few pages of sheet music in front of him and tried to focus on playing accompaniment for this man's audition. As he played, Jim's heart pounded hard to the song. He was feeling undeniable conviction from the Lord.

He hadn't wanted to be there, but they'd needed someone musical to lead auditions. Jim had no doubts that the play was just what God wanted to happen that spring in Elizabethtown. He believed, too, that it would be a powerful and profound work of God in the end. In fact, Jim was one of the first and few people with whom Phill Stumpf shared his vision for the play years ago, and Jim had supported it all along. It wasn't that Jim wasn't cheering for them.

But honestly, Jim was swamped and saw no way that he could realistically take part in the play. Being pastor of Elizabethtown Alliance Church meant an always full to-do list, and on top of that, his family had just adopted a sixteen-year-old Ukrainian boy. His new son's transition into the family wasn't going nearly as smoothly as they'd hoped, so between his work and the intensity of his home life, Jim just didn't have any energy left over for the play. Jim was a lover of storytelling with a background in drama, so he might have been a perfect addition to the cast...under different circumstances. But it was the wrong timing for him. He couldn't commit to anything extra, especially anything so time-consuming as play practices.

Still Jim had thought he felt God telling him on a couple of occasions that he belonged in the role of John. He had this sense one evening when he was helping rework the beginning of the play script (which he didn't exactly have the time for, either, but he'd agreed to help). God led him from mulling over the script in his office to sitting at that very same piano in the church sanctuary, where the Lord helped him quickly compose a few songs. The play was lacking music at that time, and Jim knew that two songs he wrote that night, *Mary's Lullaby* and *The Scribe's Song*, would be used in the performance—and they were. He finished and went home, apologized again to his wife for the late hours, and hoped he'd done all he was meant to do for the play.

But now this heavy feeling of conviction was telling him he wasn't finished. *How, Lord? I just don't know how I can add anything else to my plate right now. My family needs me at home. How can I take time away from them?* The feeling persisted through several more auditions, so Jim decided to test what he was feeling. When an auditioning actor needed someone to read a scene with him, Jim offered to read the part of John, while the actor played the scribe.

Yes, this felt right. This enormous, impossible commitment to the role of John felt like what God was saying to do.

Jim knew God wasn't letting up. He still was unsure how he could take on a role, but he decided to be open and obedient. At the end of the auditions, all he could muster up was, "I could play a part if you guys need someone." Taking this timid but faithful step made him feel a great deal of relief.

By the end of January, Pastor Jim had said yes to playing John. To stay faithful to his family's needs, though, he didn't attend weekday practices like the other actors did, and instead limited his practicing to Saturdays. The play leadership agreed to this, and Jim felt that this compromise made it do-able, maybe. He tried to focus on the highlight of the role: it was John who would explain the gospel to the audience at the end of the play.

The next month, Pastor Jim met with a mentor of his, and they decided together that it was time to start praying more aggressively for his family's needs. They prayed hard together five days a week, asking God for a drastic change in his home's atmosphere, for the enemy's defeat, and for spiritual breakthrough in his newest son's heart. God granted this! Almost immediately the issues in his home went away. There was no question that this was God honoring their prayers. And a side benefit to the relief everyone felt at home was that Jim was better able to do his part in the play.

God hadn't called him to the passion play without making it possible for him.

———

The day of the passion play was a Sunday, and that morning Pastor Jim stood before his congregation and spoke to them about taking steps of faith. That's how Jim viewed his part in the play: it was a step of faith, and a nearly missed opportunity. The best part of the role of John, after all, was that John was to explain the significance of the Passion at the end of the play. This part thrilled him! Really, it was what had helped him consent to playing the role. And yet—now that the day had come and he knew he'd be presenting Christ's gospel in front of hundreds—potentially thousands—of people that evening, he honestly felt a little frightened. In humility he ended his sermon by asking if the church would pray for him right then and there, that God would use him well when it came time to preach. Of course, the elders were glad to surround Pastor Jim and pray boldly over him.

Their prayers encouraged him, but still Jim felt nervous that afternoon on High Street, when all the cast and crew were busy making preparations for the play. He stepped away from the bustle for a moment, and wandered down an alleyway past the Lutheran church's cemetery. All alone, he told God his fears.

Lord, how am I going to pull this off?

Jim sensed a reply: *I will speak through you.* This was the reassurance Jim needed. It was God's message to deliver, after all!

When the play's action concluded and it was time for Jim to address the crowd, he looked at all the sober faces standing there in the gray, drizzly weather, ready to hear. They weren't moving despite the rain, and all their focused eye contact told him they weren't missing a word. So Jim took his time, speaking to the onlooker who was unfamiliar with the gospel, and to those who might find all of this too familiar, yet weren't truly following Christ yet. The message flowed easily and naturally, and Jim knew God was speaking through him, just as he'd promised a couple of hours before. When he was finished, Jim felt satisfied that he'd said exactly what God had wanted him to say.

To think he'd nearly missed this chance!

Yes, being a part of the passion play those past several months had been a bit of a strain and a stretch for him personally, and at times, just another task on his lengthy to-do list. But what an honor God had given him to preach before thousands there on High Street in the misty rain that day! Jim thanked God for being so patient to draw him into this role, even in spite of all his resisting.

———

Two weeks later at a mutual friend's wedding, Phill approached Jim. Phill had a mischievous look on his face, and seemed like he could barely contain some piece of news.

"Hey, Jim. I gotta admit something to you. We were just so happy to see you playing the part of John. We weren't going to tell you, but...when we wrote John's lines, we were thinking of you the whole time. Actually, the truth is, we were praying for months that you'd take the part!" But it hadn't just been the scriptwriters' hope that Jim would play John. It had been God's plan, and He hadn't neglected to give Jim everything he needed.

ACT I
Scene 2

JOHN

(addressing scribe)
What have we covered so far?

SCRIBE

(reading through the parchment)
You and your brother were cleaning your nets when Jesus came up to you and said, "Follow me." Then, you just up and left your father Zebedee in the boat! Man, I would've loved to have seen that!

JOHN

(smiling in recollection)
Yep... I couldn't believe he was talking to me when he told me to follow. I followed him for three years. He was...and is, the most amazing person I have ever met. So gentle, yet strong. So wise and somber and yet, at times playful too. And what a teacher! No one could resist listening to him. When he taught, people just stopped in their tracks. In fact, they would travel for days on end to come hear him teach. He used these incredible stories and pictures that just made so much sense. I had never heard anyone teach like he did. He had this authority when he spoke that just left you in awe. Well, all except for the Pharisees. They always had something negative to say to him, it seemed. But I cannot tell you how many times he would

answer their question or tell a story and totally confound the whole lot of them. They just didn't know what to do with him. And the miracles! Oh, my. I could tell you so many stories. Miracle upon miracle upon miracle.

<u>ACT III</u>

Scene 2: Finale

SCRIBE

(in awe)
What just happened?

JOHN

(addressing the crowd)
Do you know what just happened?

(JOHN preaches the Gospel.)

Chapter Ten
Phill
The Wrap Up

For Phill, the day of the passion play was quite a scramble. With a venue that's a public place and normally filled with heavy traffic, there can be no setting up in advance. Set up that day was a blur, as Phill ran around overseeing all the details of the play's set, sound system, and electricity, meanwhile answering a hundred last-minute questions as they came up. Phill helped the sound team find the best possible places to run their wires, as well as the best spot for the sound equipment's "home base." He handed out wireless microphones to the cast and chorus, and made sure each microphone was working properly. The bubble machine had to be set up with an extension cord running to the generator behind the first stage, not to mention the crosses needed to be raised and the enormous tomb put in place. From the time the city blocked off traffic, they had only five hours to prepare!

Phill was still rushing here and there, doing administrative things, when Pastor Jim called him away from his to-do list. The text message from Jim read, "You really need to come down here and experience this. This is pretty cool." It was only an hour until showtime, but Phill trusted Jim, and he went.

Phill knew where he'd find Jim and most of the cast and crew. It was dinner-time now, and they'd filled the seats under the tent, where they gratefully ate from a spread of donated burgers, fried chicken, and hearty potluck dishes. The meal was quite a blessing after the very physical work they'd just done, and a much-needed chance to rest from their frenzy. Phill pulled up a folding chair at a back table, beside Pastor Jim, and right away he understood why Jim had called him over. Phill sensed that God was there with them in the tent.

An hour before Phill joined them, Donna, the director, had asked the group, "How did this event change you?", and the microphone had since passed through many hands. Phill had missed most of the stories and prayers, but he made it there in time to hear one last testimony. A nineteen-year-old young man named Ethan took the microphone and stood beside his chair.

Ethan mumbled and fidgeted with his camouflage hat, and at last told how his mother had pushed him to be involved in the passion play—but he hadn't been interested. In all honesty, he'd been plummeting spiritually. His acting role was young John the apostle, and he'd only agreed to it out of obligation. It was ironic, really, how he'd been preparing with this group to tell Christ's story to the town, and meanwhile was feeling pretty unsure about his faith, or whether he could see proof of a real God in his life. Inside him had been a great deal of doubt.

His admission wasn't exactly a shock to the others. Ethan hadn't hid his feelings very well in the beginning. He'd been disruptive and stubborn during play practices, to the point that the leadership would have had good reason to dismiss him from the play, except that they chose to love and disciple him instead.

For Phill, whenever there had been conflict within the group, he'd felt strongly that the biblical answer was to disciple—not shun, shame, or punish the offender. How happy he was now as he listened to Ethan telling his story, and thanking Donna and the others for not giving up on him. Everyone who'd worked alongside Ethan had persisted in loving him despite his attitude. It had taken a few months, but through the cast God had loved and lured Ethan back to himself. Ethan's faith was strong again. Now, by choice, he was reading his Bible, praying, and gathering with other believers at church each week.

Everyone already knew Ethan wasn't the same guy who trudged into the first practice, but how thrilling it was to hear the whole story from his lips! When Ethan handed off the microphone and sat back down, someone closed by praying aloud for the performance. Phill bowed his head and knew in that moment that his view of ministry had completely changed. Their months and months of hard work had been for the people of Elizabethtown who didn't know Jesus yet. Ministering to these people had been their sole focus. All along, though, God had also been ministering to the people already part of His church, who need discipleship and love just the same.

Wow, Phill thought. *God is real...and alive... and powerful. If we keep our eyes open, we'll see all the ways he's working.* This moment in the tent burned in Phill's memory, much like the scene from the first passion play Phill ever saw. And to think that Phill's original vision for a passion play in Elizabethtown had started all of this! His vision had been the catalyst that eventually led to Ethan's change of heart, and a hundred other trickle-down workings of God. It was a humbling kind of honor.

Three hours later when the performance was over, Phill was working to clean everything up, and someone approached him, asking, "Excuse me, sir. Are you part of the passion play? This man over here wants to accept Christ." Phill had assigned specific people to help with those who had questions, and he'd expected to be free once again to oversee tasks. But again God was calling him out of task mode to something more meaningful. After Phill had answered this middle-aged man's sincere, soft-hearted questions about the drama he'd just seen, and after Phill had guided him in a prayer toward God, again he didn't regret that he'd gotten off-task. For Phill, helping this man in the moment he chose to follow Christ was the highlight of the entire day. Glory to God!

I planted, Apollos watered, but God gave the growth. So neither he who plants nor he who waters is anything, but only God who gives the growth. He who plants and he who waters are one, and each will receive his wages according to his labor. For we are God's fellow workers. You are God's field, God's building.

I Corinthians 3:6-9

Conclusion

Why was the Elizabethtown Passion Play worth the work to those involved? Why did they sacrifice their down-time, their evenings and Saturdays, for play practices and prayer meetings? Why did these Christians collaborate the way they did for months, and devote themselves to making the show go on despite every hurdle?

Because of Jesus Christ. Because of the power of his gospel for salvation to everyone who believes. Because he is real, and loving, and because following him and becoming more like him is our highest calling on earth and our most profound purpose.

May you know these truths from your own experience too.

If you confess with your mouth that Jesus is Lord and believe in your heart that God raised him from the dead, you will be saved. For with the heart one believes and is justified, and with the mouth one confesses and is saved. For the Scripture says, "Everyone who believes in him will not be put to shame." For there is no distinction between Jew and Greek; for the same Lord is Lord of all, bestowing his riches on all who call on him. For "everyone who calls on the name of the Lord will be saved." How then will they call on him in whom they have not believed? And how are they to believe in him of whom they have never heard? And how are they to hear without someone preaching? And how are they to preach unless they are sent? As it is written, "How beautiful are the feet of those who preach the good news!"...So faith comes through hearing, and hearing through the word of Christ.

Romans 10:9-15,17

And Jesus came and said to them, "All authority in heaven and on earth has been given to me. Go therefore and make disciples of all nations, baptizing them in the name of the Father and of the Son and of the Holy Spirit, teaching them to observe all that I have commanded you. And behold, I am with you always, to the end of the age."

Matthew 28:18-20

And the Word became flesh and dwelt among us, and we have seen his glory, glory as of the only Son from the Father, full of grace and truth.

John 1:14

ACKNOWLEDGEMENTS

First I must thank my father-in-law, Lee Kerr, who has known Phill Stumpf for ages. It was their friendship that provided my connection to all these dear people in Elizabethtown. After several people had said there should be a book written about the Elizabethtown Passion Play, it was Lee who finally suggested a writer to them (me!). Thanks for believing I was capable and right for the task. The task was right for me too.

Thanks to Phill and Laura Stumpf, who made it their business to provide amazing meals in their home, to introduce me to everyone who could potentially tell me a good story, and to facilitate all the interviews. On top of that, you were never skeptical toward me as a writer. Instead you trusted that God had dropped me into your lap, as he had so many other important details of the passion play. You two are godly, wonderful, and kind!

Thanks to Ed Zeager, who built my faith for the miraculous and made me want an obsession with God, like his.

Thanks to everyone who generously shared their personal stories with me: Rob Bustin, Phill Stumpf, Ed Zeager, Bob and Donna Harris, Nikky

Lewis, Pastor Jim Moynihan, Deb Garber, Brian and Lisa Harper, Larry and Erin Hodgson, Andy Tonsager, Andrea Hoover, Jack Bezares, Pastor Al Frank, Pastor Doug Lamb, Chelsea Becker, Sonya Pena, Matthew Cassidy, Ben League, and Dave Miller. Many, many thanks to you all for being so open and willing to help with this project! There could be no story without your stories.

Thanks to my son, Steel, who was only eight months old when we began the interviews, for sitting and jabbering and tolerating the process. His sweet little impatient cries are in the background of all my recorded interviews! But truly, he did great.

Thanks to my mom, Diane McGalliard, who read each chapter as I finished it, and served as my pre-editing editor. You really have a knack for picking out my mistakes! Consider editing as a future career... Thank you to my other kind friends who were willing to provide feedback.

Thanks to fellow artists Kitti Murray, Emily Tomko, and Ned Bustard, all published authors who encouraged me in the writing process.

Thanks to my editor Paul Schwarz and to my graphic and layout designer George Weis.

Thanks to my husband, Sean, who gives the best pep talks, and whose confidence in my gifting goes a long way.

Throughout the process of writing this book, I felt very strongly convinced that telling these stories was my assignment from God. I am still convinced, and am glad we don't serve Him in a vacuum. Thank you all for your contributions!

ABOUT THE AUTHOR

Rachel Kerr has a degree in English and Biblical Studies from Toccoa Falls College. She is an active member and women's ministry planner at Wheatland PCA in Lancaster, Pennsylvania. In her lifetime she has experienced many different Christian communities and denominations, and especially misses her time spent working for a Christian inner-city nonprofit. Still, she is no stranger to spiritual highs and lows, and even what she terms "spiritual angst"—yet the Lord has never let her go. As she entered into the stories from the Elizabethtown Passion Play, she felt God renewing her faith once again.

Rachel spends her days caring for her two small children (Steel, 3; and Starlett, 1) and trying to match their energy! She gets excited about psychology, great landscapes, and natural health. She is a long-time lover of creative nonfiction, and you can follow her blog at rachelkerr.wordpress.com.